Heaven Invading Hollywood

by Joshua Mills

Heaven Invading Hollywood
 Unless otherwise noted, all scripture references are from the King James Version of the Bible, copyright © 1979, 1980, 1982 by Thomas Nelson, Inc., Nashville, Tennessee.

Published by:
New Wine International Press
220 Adelaide St. N.
London, Ontario, Canada N6B 3H4
www.NewWineRevival.org

ISBN 0-9780055-1-1

Cover design and layout by Marixa Stewart
Inside pictures from NWI Image Library and public domain
Back cover photography of Joshua Mills by Mark Robert Halper – Los Angeles, CA.

For information regarding publicity for author interviews contact the publisher directly at the above address.

Printed in Canada
For Worldwide Distribution

Thank You

To my beautiful and faithful wife Janet, and my amazing son Lincoln.

To my Pastors Karl & Cheryl Thomas who have always been an encouraging support to this ministry.

To the prophetic voices which have declared God's word and blessing over my life in recent days; James Arreak, Peggy Cole, Faytene Kryskow, Patricia King, Jane Lowder, Joe & Dani Meyering, Steve Meyering and Connie Wilson. I love you all.

And to our Partners In The Glory.

"I have found the greatest power in the world is the power of prayer"

— Cecil B. DeMille

Contents

CHAPTER ONE

A Visit To Heaven

I arrived into San Francisco late on a Wednesday night in October. I was there to preach and minister at a prophetic gathering along with others in Pacifica, California. I was looking forward to these meetings but nothing could have prepared me for the wonderful things that I was about to experience that week.

I laid myself down to sleep and a few hours later I was awakened by my three Angels. I had seen them before and knew their names, but it surprised me that they had come into my room once again. It had been a long time since I had seen them. They told me that they had been sent by God and that they were going to take me to heaven.

Immediately, I was in the Spirit and I went to heaven. Many of the things that I saw, heard and experienced that night are unspeakable (2 Corinthians 12:4). I wouldn't be able to say enough to describe the beauty and awesomeness of all that I beheld. These things are too precious to cheapen by using earthly terms. But there is one thing in particular that I feel a release to share. I felt a release to share it immediately upon returning to earth that night.

When I was in heaven I was taken to a large room where the Lord presented me with a large folded piece of paper. On the outside of this paper their were words that were written which said: *"Map Of The Stars"*. It looked like the kind of maps you would purchase in a Hollywood souvenir shop to go and visit the movie stars homes.

I was instructed to open up this map, and upon doing so I realized that this wasn't a map of celebrity homes, but it was an outline of the state of California. At once tiny little lights, which appeared in form as small bright stars, began appearing in front of my eyes all over this map.

These stars appeared over Northern California and over Southern California. The desert and mountain areas began to be covered with stars. The large and small communities were covered with these bright lights. From north to south, and east to west, these lights were being turned on all over California. I could see them all the way from Sacramento, San Jose, and San Francisco to Los Angeles and San Diego. These cities were all covered with these bright stars. *"Wait a minute!"* I thought to myself. *"Los Angeles! I can see clusters of stars forming over Los Angeles. I can see stars forming all over the Hollywood area – Burbank, Glendale, Studio City, Beverly Hills, Culver City and West Hollywood."* I could see the largest concentration of stars forming all over the Entertainment districts of Los Angeles.

As I stood there astonished the stars continued to appear and they shone with great brightness. The only thing I understood from seeing this map was that the glory of God was breaking out all over the state of California. I saw something glorious breaking out. I saw these tiny heavenly lights as being the manifestation of God's glory upon the earth. These stars appeared to be portals of glory opening over California with a release of the heavenly realm.

CHAPTER TWO

Map Of The Stars

The following day after experiencing this divine visitation, and being carried away to be shown the "heavenly lights" over the state of California, the San Francisco Chronicle newspaper published a story about unusual lights being seen in the skies above the entire state. What an amazing confirmation of the things I had seen the Lord show me while I was in the Spirit.

I wasn't able to see these supernatural heavenly lights appearing in the California skies in the natural, because I was watching them being turned on in the heavenly realm. I had been in Heaven watching it happen!

We didn't know about this newspaper article until a few days later when a well known prophet from Asia came to minister at the conference and He brought it to our attention. He didn't even know at that time what the Lord had been showing me.

The following article appeared on Thursday, October 27th, 2005 as a Chronicle Staff Report in the San Francisco Chronicle. It was accompanied by full color photographs.

***

Strange Lights Reported All Across State

Residents across California and people as far east as Las Vegas reported seeing strange lights in the sky late Wednesday, according to Vandenberg Air Force Base on the central coast.

Base command staff at Vandenberg, Travis and Edwards Air Force Bases said there were no military aircraft in the sky that would have caused the lights. The Air Force bases also said there were no test missile launches Wednesday. Such tests have, in the past, resulted in light patterns that can be seen across the California coast.

The bases did not send aircraft to check on the reports of lights.

The Federal Aviation Administration's West Coast office had no reports of the lights and no aircraft were unaccounted for.

San Francisco resident Tim Sinclair said the lights appeared to be near the cross at the top of Mount Davidson Park. Sinclair, who lives near the park, described them as a series of solid lights that appeared to be hovering. When viewed through binoculars, the lights appeared to vibrate, he said.

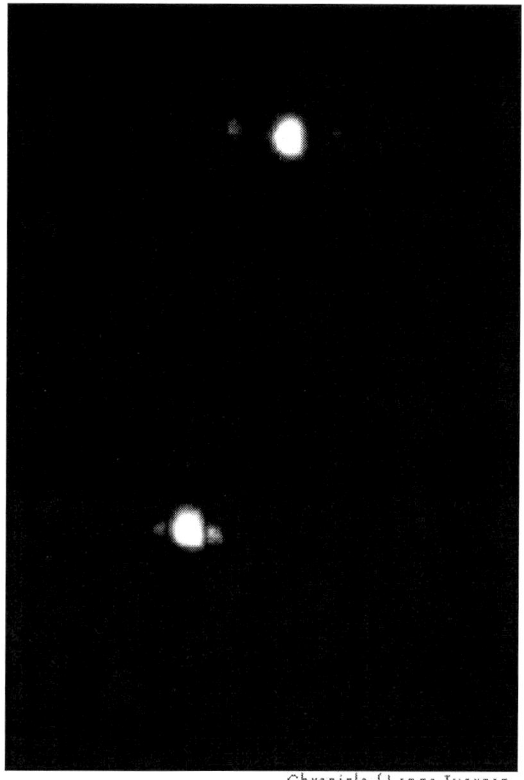

Chronicle / Lance Iversen

Unidentified lights appear to hover over San Francisco Bay, north of the San Francisco Airport, Wednesday night. The lights mimic each other's movements. Chronicle photo by Lance Iversen. (1 of 3 photos which appeared in the *San Francisco Chronicle* – Thursday, October 27, 2005). Photo by Lance Iversen.

CHAPTER THREE

Swirlings Of Glory

During the next few days of the Prophetic Gathering we began seeing other manifestations of God's presence being released as the revelation of His glory was being revealed. In almost every meeting there was a woman who had beautiful supernatural oil that would drip from her hands as the glory increased. That oil carried the fragrance and presence of God. This same lady was taken away in the Spirit several times over the course of a few days experiencing glorious visitations of the heavenly realm.

A golden glory from heaven appeared in the meetings along with Angel feathers that would visibly manifest and fall freely from mid air. In those meetings alone at least two dozen people were taken away to the Throne Room of heaven. Many came back telling of seeing Jesus Christ, heavenly visions, Angelic encounters and other glorious things.

One night while we were experiencing a strong presence of the Holy Spirit all of the electricity in the entire city of Pacifica went out without explanation. There was a darkness which came over the city in the natural realm without the lights and power being available, but the glory of the Lord grew in intensity around us as we worshipped. We knew it was the power of God – I had heard about his happening before to other people and now we were witnessing this manifestation for ourselves. It was the power of God blowing every transformer in the city made by man. Hallelujah!

"For, behold, the darkness shall cover the earth, and gross darkness the people: but the Lord shall arise upon thee, and his glory shall be seen upon thee." – Isaiah 60:2

When this happened I knew immediately that God was doing something in the realm of the Spirit, and that a shifting was taking place in the heavens. The swirlings of glory could be felt amongst us as we began to lift Him up in praise and worship. It was a beautiful thing. Again, this was another supernatural demonstration of what God was beginning to do in the realm of the Spirit. The entire hotel was experiencing a black-out along with the rest of the community, but our voices could be heard as we lifted them up to heaven ushering in another realm of glory.

Sometimes we can become so familiar with our latest technology and good inventions that we become unsettled when our earthly systems begin to fail us.

I appreciate the fact that we have great sound equipment and microphones to project our voices, and that I have the ability to play a computerized keyboard. I enjoy the sound of the electric guitar in worship and our altar ministry CDs, but I want to tell you that in this day God is calling forth a people that will become dependant upon Him solely and become familiar with the realm of the Heavens. We need to be able to worship even when everything else is taken away from us. It is time to become acquainted with heavenly things and to align ourselves with heavenly purpose.

In those moments as we were experiencing a shortage of electricity it was so precious and so wonderful. The Spirit of God was among us, and He was dwelling within the praises of His people. I could sense that at that moment the swirlings of glory were being released throughout the state of California with demonstrations of signs, wonders and miracles.

After about one hour of worshipping the Lord in complete darkness I felt an impression from the Holy Spirit that we were supposed to offer unto God a *"crossing over"* offering with our finances. God began speaking to me about going from one level of glory to the next. I wanted to participate in this and join with what God was doing, so I emptied my wallet completely and others proceeded to do the same. It was wonderful. We were worshipping the Lord with our finances, knowing that He is our provider! It was a "crossing-over" offering and God was taking us to new places in the Spirit as we were being obedient and trusting Him by faith.

When the last lady got up that night to lay her offering at the altar do you know what happened? The lights came back on and they stayed on! Again, another confirmation of what God was doing in the Spirit. We were crossing over into new places by faith, and that walk of faith was causing the lights to come on in the Spirit. Several nights prior I had seen "heavenly lights" being turned on all over the state. I believe that night opened new realms of heaven over the state of California.

CHAPTER FOUR

An Open Door

I believe that the lights I saw in heaven, and the lights that were seen in the natural all over the state of California were not only lights, but actual portals of glory. They were doors opening to the third heaven. I believe some of them have already been opened up, and others are to be opened as the revelation of His glory manifests further.

Within just a few days of having that encounter and while still ministering at the Prophetic Gathering in the San Francisco area I received an email from a Partner with our ministry and through a series of events was given an opportunity to attend a National Media Leader's Prayer Breakfast being held in Century City (within the Los Angeles Entertainment district) the following week. I knew that this was a divine connection from God.

On the day of the Prayer Breakfast I was amazed to receive preferential treatment and to be seated beside some of Hollywood's most sought after producers, directors and top filmmakers. It was a wonderful time, and most of all I felt as though God was showing me that the revelation of His glory was already beginning to manifest among the ranks of entertainment's elite.

These portals of glory that are being opened over Hollywood are divine supernatural doors for more of the miraculous and glorious in the midst of the darkness.

I want to tell you that the light of His glory shines brighter in the darkness! I praise God for the celebrities which have stood and declared their Christian values in the midst of this darkness. I praise God for Pat Boone, Dyan Cannon and Dean Jones among others who have taken a stand for righteousness in Hollywood and the secular media.

Because of the many Christians in media who have held fast in their faith, doors are being opened over Hollywood for the greatest outpouring of God's glory that the world has ever seen.

"Lift up your heads, O ye gates; and be ye lift up, ye everlasting doors; and the King of glory shall come in." – Psalm 24:7

This is the world famous **Grauman's Chinese Theatre** on Hollywood Boulevard, where many major motion pictures hold their opening night gala premieres. The first movie to ever be screened in this theatre was Cecil B. DeMille's *"The King Of Kings"* – the story of Jesus Christ from before the cross to His resurrection.

The legendary **Forecourt Of The Stars** with its famous footprints and signatures located in front of **Grauman's Chinese Theatre**.

Janet Mills poses in front of a star on the famous **Hollywood Walk Of Fame.** The Walk Of Fame features many stars of Actors, Actresses and entertainment personalities, some of which have professed their faith in Jesus Christ.

THE HOLLYWOOD SIGN

Originally constructed in 1923 as a promotional concept to launch a prestigious 640 acre subdivision – Hollywoodland – at the end of Beachwood Canyon, the ***"Hollywood Sign"***, positioned atop Mount Lee (the highest peak in Los Angeles) in the Hollywood Hills is most likely the world's most recognizable sign.

In 1978 the original sign needed an overhaul carrying a pricetag of a quarter million dollars. Each individual letter on the sign was sponsored by a major entertainment personality at the cost of $27,700 per letter so that a new sign could be constructed.

Throughout the years the Hollywood sign has been the symbol of "a dream come true" while in reality many people find themselves without hope or focus once their dreams of making it big in showbiz are shattered. Several people have committed suicide from jumping off of the sign, the first being Actress Peg Entwistle in 1932.

When praying for Hollywood we must remember those people who come here to make it big, but instead find disappointment and despair.

Joshua, Janet and Lincoln Mills pose together in front of this world famous landmark.

CHAPTER FIVE

God's Plan for Hollywood

"For I know the thoughts that I think toward you, saith the Lord, thoughts of peace, and not of evil, to give you an expected end. Then shall ye call upon me, and ye shall go and pray unto me, and I will hearken unto you. And ye shall seek me, and find me, when ye shall search for me with all your heart."
– Jeremiah 29:11-13

I know that God has great plans for Hollywood. I believe He wants to use the media for His glory and His fame. We have already seen this demonstrated to a degree with the success of recent films based around the scriptures. Testimonies of salvations and healings have been reported as people from around the world have watched these magnificent films.

Did you know that Hollywood was originally established as a bible based community? At the turn of the twentieth century, Horace and Daeida Wilcox (both dedicated Christians) purchased a 200-acre fig and apricot ranch eight miles northwest of Los Angeles and named it Hollywood.

The Wilcoxes migrated here from the Midwest to establish an enclave where no saloons or rowdy behavior would be tolerated and citizens could pursue their faith. This protestant community was well known for its conservative Christian values and beliefs.

In the early days the citizens of Hollywood resisted the movies, associating them with sin and lawlessness. By 1912, word of Hollywood's ideal filmshooting climate and beautiful landscape spread and at least fifteen independent studios could be found shooting around town.

Fortunately, the first feature film to be produced in Hollywood was made by a young producer named Cecil B. DeMille for Paramount Pictures. Cecil was a talented filmmaker from the east coast who was raised in an atmosphere of strong Christian beliefs with his father being an ordained Episcopalian minister. He went on to produce such wonderful faith-based features as *"The Ten Commandments", "The Sign Of The Cross",* and *"Samson and Delilah"* among others.

Within the next few years many old barns were turned into soundstages and Hollywood suddenly arose from being a sleepy little protestant community to becoming the movie capital of the world!

Samuel Goldwyn and Louis B. Mayer *(MGM Studios)*, Carl Laemmle *(Universal Studios)*, Harry Cohn *(Columbia Pictures)*, and the brothers Harry, Albert, Sam and Jack Warner *(Warner Bros. Studios)* – all Jewish in their faith – had all moved into town. Their faith in God and movies accelerated them to the top and established their studios as major motion picture factories.

Around the same time a Canadian Evangelist by the name of Aimee Semple McPherson came to town with her message of salvation and miracles. This magnificent woman of God was the first lady to ever preach a sermon over the radio on February 6, 1924 and the first woman ever to be granted a broadcast license by the FCC for her Christian programming. Those broadcasts took place from the beautiful domed church she built and pastored, Angelus Temple in Los Angeles, California.

Aimee Semple McPherson carried tremendous influence in Hollywood and was loved by the secular media as well as her church. She traveled the country holding revival and healing meetings with mighty miracles being demonstrated. At Angelus Temple some of her congregation members included such Hollywood luminaries as Charlie Chaplin (from the black and white comedies), Anthony Quinn, Agnes de Mille (Cecil's niece), and Talulah Bankhead.

On May 18, 1927 the Grauman's Chinese Theatre (now a legendary landmark in Los Angeles) made it's premier into the Hollywood spotlight with the opening of Cecil B. DeMille's *"The King Of Kings"* film – a religious movie about the last weeks of Jesus Christ before His crucifixion.

Looking at history we can see that God had His hand on Hollywood from the very beginning. The original purpose for this town was to be a Christian faith-based community. I know that God still has His eyes fixed on Hollywood and the media.

The night that I was taken to heaven and saw the *"map of the stars"* I knew that God was showing me something in relation to Hollywood. I saw God's glory being manifested all over the state of California in the form of tiny heavenly lights or what looked like bright stars. Over top of Hollywood (and by that I mean, the Entertainment regions in Los Angeles) I saw clusters of stars forming and beginning to shine! I believe these were portals of glory being opened over the Hollywood studios, executives, producers, directors, actors and actresses. I saw a shifting or changing of business as usual. I believe that there are some major transitions that God is going to bring forth in the entertainment industries. These lights that I saw are going to be turned on as people in the media are saved by the power of God, and also as spirit-filled Christians begin stepping into the media.

During the sixties and seventies Kathryn Kuhlman, who was a great woman of God and powerful healing evangelist, had a weekly television program on the CBS television network called *"I Believe In Miracles."* She also held regular mass miracle crusades at the Shrine Theatre in Los Angeles where many people were healed of all forms of sickness and disease.

I believe that there are still mantels that need to be picked up in this area. There are mantels for the supernatural and miraculous realm to be released throughout Hollywood and the media! There are mantels that will release God's glory for drawing in the "Kings" and "Queens" of the silver screen just as the scriptures proclaim.

"...Gentiles shall come to thy light, and kings to the brightness of thy rising." – Isaiah 60:3

I believe that God desires for many Christians to begin stepping into the media. It is a mission field that has been left unattended for too long. I think some Christians have been afraid because of the ungodly attitudes and morals that have been so prevalent on the airwaves, but now is the time for the revelation of God's glory to infiltrate the media. It is time to invade Hollywood with the light of His glory.

Aimee Semple McPherson declaring God's word with powerful demonstrations of the Holy Spirit in Los Angeles, California.

Angelus Temple built by **Aimee Semple McPherson** (as the home for her *International Church Of The Foursquare Gospel* denomination) and located in the Echo Park community of Los Angeles, California.

Joshua Mills at **Angelus Temple** as it stands today.

Evangelist Kathryn Kuhlman appeared regularly on her weekly television program which began broadcasting on the **CBS television network** in 1965. Along with her own program, other media exposure in Hollywood included appearances on the *Tonight Show with Johnny Carson*, *The Merv Griffin Show*, and *Dinah Shore*. Articles were also written about her ministry in People and Time Magazine along with countless newspapers.

Here **Kathryn Kuhlman** is shown ministering during a miracle service.

Hollywood is hungry for the supernatural realm. Just look at the line-up of current television shows – we see Psychics, Street Performers and weekly sitcoms that like to flaunt the demonic realm. I want to tell you that whenever there is darkness, there is always greater glory that abounds! It is time for the divine supernatural to become the ordinary in our media outlets!

"Arise, shine; for thy light is come, and the glory of the Lord is risen upon thee. For, behold, the darkness shall cover the earth, and gross darkness the people: but the Lord shall arise upon thee, and his glory shall be seen upon thee. And the Gentiles shall come to thy light, and kings to the brightness of thy rising."

– Isaiah 60:1-3

I can see the revelation of His glory breaking forth in Hollywood! The more I pray about it, and the more I spend time in His presence, the more God begins to show me all these tiny lights becoming illuminated over Hollywood.

Do you know what happens when a few tiny lights come together? They create a brilliant blaze! Jesus Christ is the light and His light is within us! Hallelujah!

The light that He's placed within us will shine brighter in the darkness. His glory is being revealed in the midst of Hollywood and it will shine brighter than any other star.

> ***"Then spake Jesus again unto them, saying, I am the light of the world: he that followeth me shall not walk in darkness, but shall have the light of life."***
> – John 8:12

CHAPTER SIX

The Blooming Desert

"The wilderness and the solitary place shall be glad for them; and THE DESERT SHALL REJOICE, AND BLOSSOM as the rose. It shall blossom abundantly, and rejoice even with joy and singing: the glory of Lebanon shall be given unto it, the excellency of Carmel and Sharon, THEY SHALL SEE THE GLORY OF THE LORD, and the excellency of our God… the eyes of the blind shall be opened, and the ears of the deaf shall be unstopped. Then shall the lame man leap as an hart, and the tongue of the dumb sing: for in the wilderness shall waters break out, and streams in the desert. And the parched ground shall become a pool, and the thirsty land springs of water: in the habitation of dragons, where each lay, shall be grass with reeds and

rushes. And an highway shall be there, and a way, and it shall be called The way of holiness"
– Isaiah 35:1-2,5-8

I believe that sometimes we can look at what is taking place on the earth in the natural realm and get an understanding of what is happening in the realm of the Spirit. This past year we saw many earthquakes take place all over the world – in Indonesia, United States and Japan to name only a few countries, and by this we understand that there is both a natural and spiritual shaking taking place.

Something amazing and astonishing also happened this past year in the desert places of California. Actually, it took place in Death Valley which is the driest location in the United States of America.

Flower seeds which had been left deposited on the desert floor for one hundred years because of the dry temperatures in the valley began to bloom this past year because of the rains that fell in the springtime. They are calling it the bloom of the century! Isn't that amazing?! One hundred years of nothing but dry heat and along comes a rain this year which causes these seeds to spring forth in a beautiful bloom!

The last time this happened was one hundred years ago. This story made headlines all over the world and was reported in both the Los Angeles Times and The New York Times to only mention a few newspapers. People traveled from all parts of the world to see these flowers.

The ***"Bloom Of The Century"*** – this tiny flower blossomed after one hundred years of it's seed laying dormant on the desert floor in Death Valley.

Again, I believe that this is a natural manifestation of what is taking place in the Spirit realm. Do you remember what happened in the Spirit realm one hundred years ago? Do you remember what happened in Los Angeles, California one hundred years ago?

It all started in February 1906 at the tiny home of Richard and Ruth Asberry located at 214 North Bonnie Brae Street in Los Angeles. A black preacher named William Seymour had come to town and needed a place to preach, so the Asberry's opened their home to him. The meetings were interracial, involved women and allowed regular people to minister. This was all very controversial at the time (but God is no stranger of controversy!). The meetings continued and on April 9th, 1906 Edward Lee and Jennie Evans Moore began speaking in tongues as they were filled with the power of the Holy Spirit! It began to spread like wildfire, and soon the crowds could no longer fit in that tiny house. The meetings moved to an abandoned warehouse building on Azusa street and the rest is history!

Just as the natural rains came down one hundred years ago in the Californian desert and brought spiritual rains which watered the earth, I believe these rains in the desert are just preceeding the greater glory to be poured out in Los Angeles once again! There is great glory for the West Coast! There is great glory for California! There is great glory for Hollywood once again!

Do you perceive it? Do you know it? Can you feel it? The swirlings of glory are twirling around and manifesting upon us. The Spirit of God is hovering over Hollywood. The heavenly lights have been seen appearing over the state. He is ready to bring forth a full blown manifestation of His glory!

"Behold, I will do a new thing; now it shall spring forth; shall ye not know it? I will even make a way in the wilderness, and rivers in the desert."

– Isaiah 43:19

CHAPTER SEVEN

How To Pray

I urge you to contend for a revelation of His glory in Hollywood. We know it is going to take place as God's people press in and contend for it to happen. The results will affect us all. Hollywood is a place where decisions are made that affect the entire world. Fashions and trends are created in this place. Movies, music, television and all forms of media are released from the major studios located there.

I believe that if we can reach up to touch heaven in this hour, we can touch Hollywood with the manifest glory of God. And if we can touch Hollywood we can touch the nations of the world.

It will not be good ideas or programs that will bring forth this transformation, but this can only happen by the Spirit of God. We need to touch heaven. We need to release the revelation of

His glory. I have seen transformation take place among the Inuit people in the Canadian Arctic. I have witnessed with my eyes the transforming power of God touch entire communities there. This is not impossible. It's not impossible in the far north, and it's not impossible in Hollywood.

I encourage you to begin praying for Hollywood today. Put it on your prayer list and let God stir you up in your inner man. Pray in the spirit, and also pray with your understanding.

Even though Hollywood is a place of extraordinary influence it is very seldom that the church ever rises up to pray for the filmmakers, producers, and celebrities in this town. Instead the church will boycott and protest against the decisions of Hollywood studios. I don't think that a boycott has ever got somebody saved, healed or delivered. If anything, it has made people angry with Christians and opposed to the Gospel of Jesus Christ. It is time that we begin operating in the love of God, and begin praying for these people.

Joshua Mills ministering God's love and glory with pop singer **Avril Lavigne** in Los Angeles, California.

Hollywood is only one miracle away from becoming a place for God's glory to be revealed in fullness. He will do it one miracle at a time. He always takes us step by step.

I encourage you to pray into this glory. Pray for Hollywood and praise God that He is changing the atmosphere. Your praise and worship will create a climate for miracles! Do it even right now.

Pray for the executives and managers of the studio empires. Pray for the directors, producers, writers and those working in the technical aspects of media. Pray for the celebrities – the actors, actresses, musicians and other notables. Pray that God will move upon their hearts and that they will be open to His leading. Pray for the Christians that are currently working in this field and that their spirits would be strengthened as they contend for righteousness in Hollywood.

I have put together some prayer points that you can use as we believe God together for a demonstration and manifestation of His glory being revealed in Hollywood!

PRAY FOR:

▪ Workers and laborers that will be obedient to go into this harvest of souls.

▪ Protection, guidance, direction and divine opportunity for Christians in the media.

Supernatural release of the revelation of His glory in their lives.

▪ Blessing upon media which contains strong Christian morals and view points. Blessing upon the studios which produce these television shows, films and productions.

▪ Salvation, deliverance and freedom for those in the Entertainment industry that do not currently know Jesus Christ as their personal Lord and Savior. Pray that their eyes might be opened to the truth of the gospel.

▪ Radical, supernatural miracles and encounters with the Holy Spirit for those in Hollywood who do not yet know Him and for those who do.

▪ Those who have lost hope and vision. That their hope might be restored through a personal encounter with Jesus Christ.

CHAPTER EIGHT

Studio Contacts

On the next few pages I have compiled a list of some of the major Hollywood area studios so that you might cover them in prayer. Use the prayer points on the previous pages for a guide as you lift them before the throne of grace. I also encourage you to write these studios a kind letter if you have been blessed by a television program, song or film with good Christian moral values. The producers and executives at these studios need to know when you are blessed by media with a positive message. You can make a difference today by supporting the work of other Christians in the media. We need to demonstrate the love of God at all times (stay away from boycott and negative mail) and remember to encourage these creative people in their good efforts.

ABC Entertainment
500 S. Buena Vista St,
Burbank, CA 91521
(808) 460-7777 ▪ www.abc.com

Capital Records
1750 N. Vine St,
Hollywood, CA 90028-5305
(323) 871-5001 ▪ www.capitalrecords.com

Castle Rock Entertainment
335 N. Maple Dr, Suite 135,
Beverly Hills, CA 90210
(310) 285-2300 ▪ www.castle-rock.com

CBS Entertainment
7800 Beverly Blvd,
Los Angeles, CA 90036-2188
(323) 575-2345 ▪ www.cbs.com

Dreamworks SKG
1000 Flower St,
Glendale, CA 91201
(818) 695-5000 ▪ www.dreamworks.com

Fox Broadcasting/Twentieth Century Fox
10201 W. Pico Blvd,
Los Angeles, CA 90035
(310) 369-1000 ▪ www.fox.com

Gener8Xion Entertainment
3400 Cahuenga Blvd,
Hollywood, CA 90068
(323) 874-9888 ▪ www.8x.com

HBO
2049 Century Park East, Suite 4100,
Los Angeles, CA 90067-3215
(310) 201-9300 ▪ www.hbo.com

Lifetime Television
2049 Century Park E #840,
Los Angeles, CA 90067
(310) 556-7500 ▪ www.lifetimetv.com

MGM Studios/United Artists
2500 Broadway St,
Santa Monica, CA 90404-3061
(310) 449-3000 ▪ www.mgm.com

Miramax Films
8439 Sunset Blvd,
West Hollywood, CA 90069
(323) 822-4100 ▪ www.miramax.com

MTV Networks
2600 Colorado Ave,
Santa Monica, CA 90404
(310) 752-8000 ▪ www.mtv.com

NBC Entertainment
3000 W. Alameda Ave,
Burbank, CA 91523-0001
(818) 840-4444 ▪ www.nbc.com

New Line Cinema
116 N. Robertson Blvd, Suite 200,
Los Angeles, CA 90048
(310) 854-5811 ▪ www.newlinecinema.com

Paramount Pictures
5555 Melrose Ave,
Los Angeles, CA 90038-3197
(323) 956-5000 ▪ www.paramount.com

Showtime Networks, Inc.
10880 Wilshire Blvd, Suite 1600,
Los Angeles, CA 90024
(310) 234-5200 ▪ www.sho.com

Sony Pictures Entertainment
10202 W. Washington Blvd,
Culver City, CA 90232-3195
(310) 244-4000 ▪ www.sony.com

Trinity Broadcasting Network
PO Box A,
Santa Ana, CA 92711
(714) 832-2950 ▪ www.tbn.org

Turner Network Television
1888 Century Park East, 14th Floor,
Los Angeles, CA 90067
(310) 551-6300 ▪ www.turner.com

United Paramount Network (UPN Television)
11800 Wilshire Blvd,
Los Angeles, CA 90025
(310) 575-7000 ▪ www.upn.com

Universal Studios
100 Universal City Plaza,
Universal City, CA 91608
(818) 777-1000 ▪ www.universalstudios.com

The Walt Disney Company
500 S. Buena Vista St,
Burbank, CA 91521
(818) 560-1000 ▪ www.disney.com

Warner Bros. Studios
4000 Warner Blvd,
Burbank, CA 91522
(818) 954-6000 ▪ www.warnerbros.com

WB Television Network
4000 Warner Blvd,
Burbank, CA 91522
(818) 977-5000 ▪ www.thewb.com

About The Author

An anointed minister of the gospel, recording artist, conference speaker and author, **Joshua Mills** worships and preaches by standing under the cloud and ministering directly from the glory unto the people. He has written over 600 songs and is known for his ability to lead people into spontaneous worship. Traveling all over North America and around the world, he has been creating a realm of glory wherever he goes, with a message that *"praise changes the atmosphere."*

Along with holding meetings in Europe, South America, Asia, New Zealand, and other nations, Joshua Mills has ministered extensively throughout the Canadian Arctic regions witnessing dramatic transformation taking place in whole communities and the lives of many Inuit people.

The Lord is working with Joshua and his wife Janet, confirming His Word with miraculous signs and wonders that testify of Jesus Christ. Along with people turning to God and finding salvation and receiving healing in their bodies, the Lord is visibly manifesting signs of His love. In all of their meetings the sweet presence of Jesus permeates the atmosphere and people's lives are changed forever.

Join us in Southern California for a

HOLLYWOOD INVASION

If you have been stirred by the message in this book, and you feel led to come and minister in the heart of movieland, we invite you to come and join us in a ***Hollywood Invasion***. During these missions we will be going into the entertainment centers of Los Angeles with the manifest presence and glory of God.

If you are interested please call or email the ministry for information about the next ***Hollywood Invasion***...

PRAISE CHANGES THE ATMOSPHERE

God has already given you the key to change the atmosphere around you. ***There's a sound in your spirit, that when released, will shake the foundations around you and bring forth miracles.*** *As you discover this you will begin praising Him in the midst of any situation or circumstance.* ***Receive your supernatural breakthrough*** *as this worship and teaching CD brings revelation from the Word of God.*

$18.00 USD/$23.00 CAD+ shipping & handling

Available online at: **www.NewWineRevival.org**

Plan now to attend our next

New Wine International

Signs & Wonders Conference

Joshua and Janet Mills welcome you to come and receive from the Heavenly realm. Several times a year they conduct conferences where people from all over the world, that are of like mind and like spirit, come to join in unity and one accord in lifting up the name of Jesus Christ! It is always a time of great blessing as you will make new connections in the glory, and meet new friends as God manifests Himself in miracles, signs and wonders. If you make time in your busy schedule to come we know that you will not be disappointed! You will be changed by the high praise, heavenly worship, revelation in the Word and power of God! You will be embraced by the love and glory of the Holy Spirit as you pursue Him and allow fresh purpose and eternal destiny to be released into your life.

For more information about the next conference visit our website or contact the ministry offices:

www.NewWineRevival.org

"Building A Realm Of Miracles & Heavenly Glory"

- Understand and become acquainted with The Heavenly Realm

- Learn how to co-operate with the pattern of heaven and create the cloud of Glory

- Begin flowing in miracles, signs and wonders

Register today to attend the next CTC Glory School!

In Canada: **NWI**, 220 Adelaide St. N.,
London, ON N6B 3H4
In USA: **NWI**, PO Box 595765, Fort Gratiot, MI 48059
(519) 672-1221 ▪ office@newwinerevival.org

Ministry Address

*If you would like to contact Joshua Mills' ministry for invitations to hold conferences or church meetings, to become a monthly **"Partner In The Glory"**, or if you have a prayer request that you would like Joshua and Janet Mills to lift up before the throne of grace, please contact the ministry at the following address.*

New Wine International Ministries
Joshua & Janet Mills
220 Adelaide St. N.
London, Ontario, Canada N6B 3H4

www.NewWineRevival.org